The Devastation

The Devastation
Melissa Buzzeo

NIGHTBOAT BOOKS
NEW YORK

ISBN: 978-1-937658-25-0

Cover photograph: Andrew Kenower, 2014

Cover Design by Timeless, Infinite Light
Interior typesetting by Margaret Tedesco
Text set in Plantin and Futura

Cataloging-in-publication data is available
from the Library of Congress

Distributed by University Press of New England
One Court Street
Lebanon, NH 03766
www.upne.com

Nightboat Books
New York
www.nightboat.org

a sea-wreck in language: PREFACE FOR A WORK UNDONE

If water is desire, connectivity, the possibility of current, language itself, what happens when that water is emptied out, when nothing is left but the basin of retrieval, the properties of the body and the memory of matter, addressed?

Further, what happens to language, to the body, when this address has disappeared? What happens to death? What happens to life—clotted, closeted and unrealized? In all this: then.

At the bottom of the sea, unidentified lovers have survived The Devastation, the water as it violently emptied, the pronouns as they disappeared into the Marine Biology of the ocean floor. Covered in decayed matter, that of the floor, that of themselves, what was once human skin, reeking of a terrible stench, the lovers repeat this one gesture: Reaching and pulling off from the other the clotted elements of the sea. The once animals, plants—this matted reach. All that is left of language in an alternate system of life. They reach and they recoil in a gesture of extreme eroticism. Extreme because it is all that is left, because it combines what is left and pushes against limit. Erotic because it is the ultimate reach: through nothing, back to one self: the other body at the limit of self. The epigraph comes from Blanchot: *"The danger that the disaster acquire meaning instead of the body."*

It began as a book that was to address healing, text after loss. As devastation often does, it became all loss and as such what to do with a language smaller and smaller, a meaning more and more totalitarian? What to do with a book enacting itself? These fields of yearning or narrative held so far apart. And further, what is the role of community in (linguistic) trauma? How to speak in the absence of address, the pre-language torn away, the mirrors broken on the floor—the form, all forms, eradicated, displaced, done away with? Abbreviated in an economy that does not weigh the silent aspect of address. The nothing aspect. Content and form held so far apart.

Where too is "voice," singular, collective damaged dreaming/dreamt, outside of language and blocked by the overcoded remnant inscription that persists past sound?

Really this book is about meaning: organic and inseparable from life. The same elements that made me leave this book in loose time urged me back to it. The torn tongues addressing themselves.

When I began this book, it was accompanied, in my reading, by the swollen singular rhythms of Jeanne Hyvrard, Marguerite Duras dissolving, works that addressed the body, that enacted healing. I wanted this—To open a blank or flooded page to rupture and release. In writing the book, in getting to the next part, I realized that this can not be done statically but only ecstatically and as such only in the time after many private and painful omissions. Thus: poetry, cross genre or what it could become. Which to me is beyond itself. In the time of blankness, the work of Bhanu Kapil was very present as silent drawn current touching. Soft filtered accompaniment. Godard was also very present here, Benjamin, and the alternative history of women herbalists. Writing about disease, cosmology. Elizabeth Grosz, Aaron Applefeld, Melanie Klein.

Watching over and over again the videos of disabled performance artist Lisa Bufano—touching—in a new and completely altered form—her words "I want to be seen as attractive and beautiful and sexy like everyone else. But I think that in my artwork, for me, it's trying to find some comfort with being everything a human can be." I wanted to copy that reach, any reach and after reading Clarice Lispector three years after the initial beginning of the book, I was finally willing to touch it unafraid, knowing that it might be just paper after all or less than paper, nothing to eat and certainly not water. Bufano and Lispector both gave me so much courage, they filled me with nothing.

Writing the last section, I went back to writers who had been so important to me before who filtered unmoored. I wanted to understand what the non meaning of this meaning meant. The impovrishment in abundance and vice versa. At 4 am each morning by candlelight in full fall, I read Christa Wolf, Ingeborg Bachmann, Hélène Cixous as I confronted death in writing, the legacy of containment. As Bachmann says: "You understand, my inflammatory letters, my inflammatory appeals, my inflammatory stance, this entire file I have put on paper with my burned hand—I'm so afraid that it could all become a charged piece of paper. Ultimately all the paper in the earth is charred by fire or melted by water, they burn fire with water."

Perhaps because or through these texts, the relationship between reader and writer is of the utmost charge in this book. It is and it is not. It is the most thing, the damaged thing disappeared. The gesture thing: survival even outside of language.

In the beginning of the book it says:

Turn the pages of my book

For someone else to do it

For you

is erotic

For the broken steps of culture

For the bereavement that is palpable

The lightness of the page, erotic

What I wish for my book now is that it be held, placed: read or unread. I wish for my emptied out earth to touch the real earth that is sometimes full, sometimes shy, that is longing. I wish to close this which has held out too long.

I am interested in the fallibility of a single image.

I write to you from the charnel ground, where I belong.

Where I wrote these words.

And cupped them.

Like the gestures of retrieving water and putting it to the mouth.

For you, who held out. Who closed. Sometimes full, sometimes shy.

If it was, then love is much more than love: love is yet before love: it is the plankton striving, and the great living neutrality striving.

—Clarice Lispector

The rags, the refuse ... not to make an inventory of these things, but to allow them, in the only possible way, to fulfill their existence.

—Walter Benjamin

A tracking shot is a moral act.

—Jean-Luc Godard

At the bottom of the sea, unidentified lovers have survived The Devastation, the water as it violently emptied, the pronouns as they disappeared into the Marine Biology of the ocean floor. Covered in decayed matter, that of the floor, that of themselves, what was once human skin, reeking of a terrible stench, the lovers repeat this one gesture: Reaching and pulling off from the other the clotted elements of the sea. The once animals, plants—this matted reach. All that is left of language in an alternate system of life. They reach and they recoil in a gesture of extreme eroticism. Extreme because it is all that is left, because it combines what is left and pushes against limit. Erotic because it is the ultimate reach: through nothing, back to one self: the other body at the limit of self.

Part One: THE FLOOR

The danger that the disaster acquire meaning instead of the body.

—Maurice Blanchot

How does one say The Devastation
When it no longer is
When I am not waiting for you writing for you
When we

are not

intact.

Impoverished speech filling this empty bed
Of sediment and debris
In such overexposed light
How does one say

Against this one tree of fragment exposure

I lift your jacket
I lift your throat, crustacean.

To substantiate shell

When we no longer are anything but these lanterns giving light
These colors abating chemicals
These elements that have been left out.

To say there are no more nutrients on the floor
In the absence of covers
That there are no more dividers
Only this white bed which grows larger and larger
Only these books that lack cover or are all cover.

No containers
A singularity that is approached and done away with
A singularity committed to memory

So stark against this speech

Turn the pages of my book
For someone else to do it
For you

is erotic

For the broken steps of culture

For the bereavement that is palpable

The lightness of the page, erotic

You start with an image: one that has been torn out of your mouth

You fold it in half: you stay.

Beside what drained
Beside what parted
Beside what had yet to be

You and I waiting
For our bellows to fill with water, for our behests and our bequeathals
For the separation and the document
That which floated away
That which was held away
In the giving of no space
Sea and wreck: beside what drained

The overexposure: particles of existence
The embrace global
And guttural.

We who can no longer say Parched throats
Water
Pure pavement

We who can no longer remember the license that ran dry
The freedom on the periphery
Your hands and waiting.
In the no longer calculable: dry.

That this can not be separate
That there is no text for mouth
No text for body
No text to follow this, run dry
That this cannot be completed outside of itself

In the absence of covers numbness and decay except for this clarity this
return

We who no longer say parched throats and remember our faces

And remember our extremities

As our bellow fills with water

Memory pushed to the extreme.

To search for so long: for the tie
That which was cut from someplace else
Brought to someplace else
To replicate being

To press this skin firmly into the future
To retrieve; broken mouth to stone
My hand low in the river of elsewhere
What has been taken
What has not been allowed

All the wading that has never been done
And the fear of separating from the start.

To call you adjacent
To hear you adjacent
I send love to the fixed place
The overturned place
That which is embanked in silence
Embarked in presence.

A tie that would replace meaning.
And to have one but not the other

To wade and to evacuate before
Skin erasure before.

In every article
In every containment
That which breaks
That which subsumes article

And the frozen book
Endless out of fear.

In the gesture towards nothing. Towards no one. Language passage
erased, the sea capsized into itself

To hold you against that
To hold us against that
They, them.
That

To stay here where there is nothing
Not even bone breaking over skin
The long haul of nothing indivisible from self
To not imagine the evacuation of yourself
This self
a prism water

Breaking over bone
As the stone once absorbed.
Beach, bequeathal before.
As language inscription bone
I can go no further than this kiss: this begun in being.

Desiring, nothing
The memory of hands
Bones breaking into branches
Clavicle memory branch

Skeletal and reconfigured from someplace else
I leave you as I wake to you.
Without language
Skeletal
A mineral presence

And the particulars that juxtaposed met.

They drew no breath
As this stay precluded only deposit, resonance

That there is no other book
Language forbidden and the return remedial.
That the rhythm cannot be found
As I hold you to weather
Can not be folded
Placed against skin
In the ancient language of
This body next to that
Where the text breaks off to no other
Folded over skin.
Correspondence or no longer
In the break of recovery
Of remembrance
In the inability to shift the pages
I make a list and it breaks off
And it binds itself

We filled our books with sand
So that they would not drain water

I can remember the periphery, the seaweed taking shape.
In what was not embankment.

The unarticulated branches
Desultory chasm, pause

The silt in the mouth of the ocean.

All forms or no form: the body taking place

Over such ravage and the one sea kept. The one sea listened too.
Lavender and leaving and secreted oils. The scent past the ocean. In the
unclaimable ravage of met.

Out of your hands
Out of the metal that binds you
The mental between.
After plunge
Outside of sound. As you enter the bloodstream and bind yourself: space.

And our near arrival
And our near discordance
Tumble placard and met
Wilting ravage and the sea.

A blood that opens
A sound that nears

Rushing to ravage a darkening deepening distilling

Everything falling through, page.

Our wingstem attacked
Our wingspan intact

The measure of the sea and the limit of the sea
The dried bones
The overturned pages
The blank bones
Measured and then missed
In this capacity for ruler and longing.
Breast and bone: the sea
I take the scales
The lingering shells
The sea weed abasement.
The rotted the rusted, the perusals of scent and exhume

Someday the oils that would cling to this page. The new patterns. Flecks
of skin. Broken off. Between skin and the page. The scales of here.
Littered off.

As so quickly this disappearance in somebody else's arms.

Dried against the shell.

I have nothing left to give
In this absence of element

As we turn as you turn as even the sand breaks off and comes back as
being

A bone so clean it is a shell
A below so bestowed
A belonging after

And the hushed abasement.

The light that comes through
The body that comes through
A shell that belongs only to air

I take my hands from the river, my strained clothes from the cover.

As we become just the take of what leaves

As each cover cries out so vapidly for salt

In all the crumbling unwritten

Lying over the fragment of the earth.

Pure parchment water

The seaweed dissolved struggling of its nutrients.
The stasis egregious

A moon shape
A glass shape

The relics over your face.

The one cell released from the many
To lift the shadow from your head.

What is brought to light but not to body

To write instead the beautiful passage the fallen pretext the etched out:
retrieval.

We dive and also have yet to dive

Presence next to presence and the falling chemicals.

I want what you want at the other side of the river

And the beds that we made

The crashing of consonants next to constants

The hard enactment of speech next to matter

And the water that is left

In future frieze of tree

The beds that we made

The cellular destruction

Cellular retrieval.

The embankment and the return
The broken gesture

Cauling.

We look at the sand. We have no other word for water.
No other when for now.

All the books other

Flushed against the ready
The resume the culture
Flushed against the resemblance
Turning

To resemble itself
The broken weight of species

The threadbare traces, treaty

All that is possible

And the binding. And the weight.

Someone must enter the inside space
In their own weight

Their own gravity

A weight flush and a depth flush, flesh: threadbare

We have yet to include that which is possible

To resume our own weight

Of pages stuck together

Of pages loosened

Turn the pages of my book

Induce gravity

And speech

The edges to spread

At arms length

At near spread

A positioning that is possible
We have our own weight to consider

And the bus
And the speed of the bus
At arms length

All the traces of the trestle
Indecipherable
Undeniable. The call of trace to trace

For someone to bind you to it
Your lips radiant
And your length radiant

Your stature redeemed

Turn the charge to include the book

Not on a stand
And not inclusion, exclusion at arms length

The wind is torn from elsewhere, this distance is not unique

There is the question of the passivity at large
The turning
The charging
The changing
At arms length

As the page is formatted to include duration division decision erasure

Duration: the trace's induction

As we spread our lips to the century

As the wind is not from elsewhere but from your arms undeniably apart.
As I wait as you wait, uncalled.

The poem that is turning to include weight

Outside the deepening air
Outside the changing spread
The culture invested in air

The duration erotic and the signs in the air

The seepage a love to consider

When all is threadbare

As we read through cheesecloth

And breakage

And love.

The residual, the culture

in love.

The flame I leave in the other room. On the table before the door. The hard door of renounce.

That flame that is left but still lit
The blue ink
The memory of birds the platelets planked inked.

Left, adjacent ajar.

So that we might uncontinue.
So that I might continue unknown alone
The hard swallow of continue.

I remember the textual city
And the meaning of met
The many words for sea
The ink on your hands
What I can't remember, recall, deliver
And the wait it in our faces
The swallowed back body
Pure fire water unable to withstand sight

A hard city table separate from table
I leave it there I leave you there so that we might recall: here.

At the bottom of. Floored

In the impossibility of getting close enough
I press against the water
Which floods absence

Our skin comes off. This does not mean we touch.
Our hands break off; we have yet to reach bottom.

To go back and forth: the unlit room the mineral
A boundary-less-ness, a sea
The meaning of embankment
That which makes freedom
That which takes it away
We found ourselves here
We reach towards the other animals
Other particles of skin.

Which has become in your mouth alone.

I couldn't say Sea and so let it join

How does one say in the absence of text
In the nothing to carry
In the everything to renounce
That I want—without article

And in the throat the tangle growing inward
The long vowels held and held
The distant chemicals of renounce.

And where is the poem that does not follow.
We forget names
But not breath
We give off a heat that is not pure

It no longer matters.

We filled our names with the book.

Our tongues with the tide

In the impossibility of growing: land or sea.

Of denouncing such magnificence caught in one word

The participle I lost to touch your skin

I followed what was formless to me.

And why did I agree to such earth
Such incremental
excrement covered
earth

To want and to be tangential to want.

In the dissolution of paper
In the disuse of paper

And the ink on the skin instead of the letter

Rotted and the entry
Thrown away

The book that comes apart in my hands. The book that is for you. And
not for you. And for a forked line. The bones held safely over the ocean.
The swelling survival above the forked line
In neither of our hands
How to direct this force
This break
And this body
You bang against the body bilingual until it breaks off
And you are not a title
And you can't be kept
And the air that is radiance breaks against you
And the sea that is permanence that is private
Overfull and breaking, longing
Over longing breaking bonding met.
My heart against this
And the unreachable met
Of the shells in the air.

The carved out space.

To open a blank or flooded page to rupture and release.

In the return to the other language
The words strained
Fractured and bent
The stiffness of the body bending over
And the inability to keep.

I wanted these words in your body
This heart in your head.

In the restraint of the other language. The gentle spillage. And the word
by word pillage

To give up caught
And catch
And have
And help

Only the covers left
The hard covers of retreat.

In the rain
And in the desire for the rain
In the return of the work

And the swollen seepage
The seismic wreckage

These arms for yours—
Bent over spilling inwards
And the catastrophe of the over language
The rain over your throat and the inability to keep cover.
Alone.

This avowal unmet
Safe over the catch of earth
The wreck that is read alone
The marks we make and the seismic here. Straining towards what

To breathe in and out
To desire in and out
The papers removed
And the pages retorn
In the leap from desire and met
In the untangling of species

The non sea and the safety valve opened
The near sea and the unraveling
And the unfolding
To fold out of being near the sea
And to break against rock.

As we keep what of breakage returns what of stone survives the book too
heavy to keep to light to lessen

And the brevity of caught
Unfolding and unmaking
For me and not for me
For you but only at a distance.
In the lightness of the page, erotic
Plunged between the covers
Loose between the covers
And rocking to sleep
On somebody else's boat
In somebody else's sleep.
Our sea and nearness
And the rock of shell breaking over body
Over book betrayal
Over one language pulling out
In the inextricable memory of being
And I am quite near the sea
In the absence of address
And the body I make for you

This strain over that

In the other memory
In the other words

In the language that won't open
In the other who won't go to sleep
In the non language of the book
And the tangled pages removed

Over bone
Over sea
Over memory of sea

The torn gravity that pulls me to here.
Against the book that is neither open nor closed
Neither seismic nor wrecked
It is too dark to see and   .

How long it took me to climb out of this body

We are bespoken by matter and as such we cannot touch.

Between us: blank line
Before us a dampness that has eradicated

Before us: blank light

To say that we have come from the same place

And how closely I resemble
that which you are not

The before text the after writing

I put my lips to yours. We try to pronounce these words: I cannot

And that we are swimmers together
That we miss the page
And that we are swimmers together

All this language in my throat
All this emptying out of language

On the floor sometimes, spines of gold.

In striated cells of longing.

We hold the particles of water up to the light

How can one say The Devastation when it no longer is.
When we no longer are.
Beside it.

The nekton (swimming)
The plankton (drifting)
in the overlying water
Crustacean
Pelagic

This hard glow next to meter

On ancient paper: we swam to each other

On ancient paper: as we are to each other.

Demolished
measured net

And this is my way of staying connected to you outside this singular length.
My body or both our bodies.

At arms length, at throat tide: this disbelief.

To want and to want and to want
And to have no recourse towards want.

In this place of no roots
To complete the exhaustion

Between the two notebooks, neither one breaking neither one buried.
The tissue paper
The sight one to the other
The translation buried

And the transition brought to light
The covers collected, returned
What one page collects of another.
And the seeing through paper
And the never to be held
The last place
And the first room
The white walls collapsing.

Here the walls make paper and also I make paper.

In the uneartherd garden the open time

And at first to encounter the sea.

Sometimes we hear words lining the littoral

Sometimes our hands undo the absence

Sometimes we remember the properties of matter

And as such we cannot touch

The portions the sky took of our mouthes.

Still the hand breaches: survival
Still the harvest speaks to itself.

I want wrought iron and the sea—

The earth trying to substantiate arrival.
To subsume bequeathal.

And can we call it a lost language

The translation redundant
And bound to water

It is because we remember the water of before that we take our hands to skin.

To have never left: this broken text.
That we fold over skin.
I had set out to write about the cold
The frozen freeing of form
But it no longer existed
But we no longer existed
This harsh formlessness over skin

How does one say of the Devastation
When it no longer is

That I made the bed with the book

That I had to unmake the bed to remove the book

To remake the self

All the remnants of the drained text leaking in another language.

A text outside of text
A room outside of room

Between the two notebooks: the unaltered page.

To be unable to pronounce: evaporant

As I did before.

A compression of all the other books,
An evacuation of all the other books.

This seed placed open where no sound can reach it.

brittle stars, basket stars.

The exhaustion of substance
For,
dead.

Words were turning gold in the black sun of silence.

Buried in the sea-bed
In swimming or drifting forms
In the overlying water
In pelagic communities
The radical symmetry
The return

All the other words for sea

When the adventure has reached its farthest point where the sea listens only to the sea, writing suddenly appears as a broken coastline which no map records.

The bodies against the stone

Drawn.

The bodies cast into the sea.
I give you this marked stone.

And the water rose from the middle
And the sound followed the sea
No trace of blood.

And then there were no more notebooks
Because there was no more pre text
The blue was gone
Like her brown
Bright in the market
Wind song
In the blue the grey the wind
The embroidered saris
The paper from Nepal
From India
Paper
someone
touched

The plain school notebook prairie
The notebooks of rhythm and refusal
All bound together
Into nothing
Which stood as one

Part Two: AN OBJECT

What is this falling into the silence of the poem. What is beauty that falls? And what is left of the poem after its ruin?

—Giorgio Agamben

If it were not so separate if something had been saved I would give you a piece of The Devastation now, here. Not like a text, like an object.

I would break it off.

Part Three: THE SKY

THE FIRST DAY

Against stone what is caught there
In the absence of water
In the everything to demand

Fish caught and heavy
We traded our organs for stones
Our water for entry
Our mouths for the pleasure of the default paint.

What is buried in the other body.
I want to be built there.

How a book looks left
How a finger looks caught
How a book sags left

After three years of non address
After partition
Size and matter
All the hearts beating in different states away
All the paint privately addressed

The nudity set to fall
The frigidity set to free

I wanted to collect that which was not there
The size of the park
The ocean in a hand, yours
The teacup in your stomach

The four soggy books barricading the drain.
Eradicating the drain
Coming to claim it caught

Variations of this of that of the house on fire or the lawn. Or the
heart the entry.

Variations of vandalism
And the park
The night '
The creeping out of Serbia, Albany night
From wire to wire from pole to pole
What can be made that isn't caught.

And you break it you build it you break it in half store the halves
The seismic met.

The coming undone of the knot
The feeling that you are bound to close

The coming undone of the boundary

And then a small path

And then stone by stone

You follow the stones out the unbearable stones

The stone that are irregular shaped

Pattered pleasure

She wears a bag around her head

The air is clenched

The necklace is given

The disc is taken

The foreign is met

In someone else's body

Identity crashing and wired

And then the black out which satisfies everybody.

Our want for entry

To be so tired of one's own language

To haul the jug the bundle to not drink this other water.

Our when for want

Our name for treaty

The word for fall

In the well

After the blackout everything was given. There were no lights
but still we repeated thus. There are no lights. There is clench
and seize. Size. There is the rolled up bed the rolled up wall. The
splattered paint. The carpet that won't unfold. Pockets of water
that won't fold that breathe their own water season size. Water to
water earth to earth the globe arranged as falling aching untied.

In the matter there was water but not here.

In the ocean there was swimming but not then.

Ragged and rubble and lingering doubts: rebuild.
The immensity of the cost
The failure to calculate
The drainage of the rest

Still we repeated thus.

At great cost I climbed over the alternate rubble. In the blanked
out space the pure hole. An accident that stayed rebuild. In the
pure cost the whole. Linger and free. A lantern punched with
stars. A non star a tree. Without holes.

In the well there was build in the room there was rest. A stripped
bed. A body naked no longer young pulsing or read. A stacked book.

A staid life. Ragged and free.

Still we repeated thus
When language no longer multiple
Leave come door when
Floor
How to say what happened to you.

Your want was big
Your season was tried
Your life was balloon parachute and tie.
Parachute tie silk
You punctured the air
You would not drain being
It was expensive.

You slept on the floor
You wove your pockets into memory.
You stayed on the floor
The floor did not fit
It was a long day a long night that continued as just one letter
And then stopped.

It must have been on the next to last day I slept on the bed.

Restless heated forced out
To force your body through a chain
A circle a body.

On the last day where the books had been. Heated waste.
August and all undone.
August and all arranged
And IIIIIIIII

There is no heart that beats like that.

Narrative swollen punctured vandalized huge. What the letter could miss.
How to say waste
How to say garbage how to say I grabbed your throat and tore the globe.
In the water there was waste
Did I drain it.

What will not be punctured what stayed to close.

You get on airplane to nothing to nowhere. You touch sky you
touch down. You wander in the blank air. On the book you write

the sky. In the sky you read address. The air catches the plane forces. *Stages of Dying* by Elisabeth Kübler-Ross. Pages 1-58. Airplane.

You touch down. You return. You repeat.
I came here to learn to breathe. You breathe you repeat you die repeating.

In the air there is a sign in the water such waste.

The lavender in that throat the oil in that hair the arms in that entry
Our names signed ready.
What was the fault line
Whose was it.
What left what buried what tried to close.

How to speak about something that contains nothing.
You force your start
You lay on the floor the fountain the water the waste.
You are pressed and stretched, stoned in.
Many visions as it is said an airplane to no where and then a
pause and then some magic and then some rubbing oil and the
story entire.

You get back on the plane. With your umbrella your jugs of water. Your writing your when. Curtains instead of the wall instead of the page.

It is now that I was leaving.

You are cried at
Meaning is offered
You are hugged at
Meaning is taken

Without an umbrella what stands to close.

The fault line was always ready. You heave. Breath to breath and line.

You follow the line

One narrow vision
One forlorn tunnel
One jagged curve

One could say a dump but no it's the library
The throat closing filling in its own line.

You are bruised at you are bothered at.
For a while you try tent
For a mouth offering
For a body?

I was wrapped in oils. In my head down my sternum as I lay
blank page.
I was doused in shade

It was so soft in that vapor

The plane the phone the jagged line.
The mirror broke
The placement broke
The walls are very thin
Your body did not fit between the cracks the walls the when.

Heavy body
Bloated mirror
Parquet floor.

How to speak about stop without ruining your eyes.
There was newspaper.
A mosaic in speech but how to catch it touch it.

There was the limit which you slept with
There was the license which you slept with
In the bed no longer a book
It became too big
It became too small
It became listed
As someone else's article.

The phone rang the vapor salted the mirror ran the ground
shifted the pages flew a cliché you say again and again. The
desire books drained their tears. Tennis started and an election
and a rain a soft rain. A soft and desperate rain rung in chemicals.

How to speak of something that contains nothing.

An empty body
A snow walk
An empty shoe
A licensed body
A stolen shoe.

Did you drain the plane here. Here to here.
Did you draw it in a notebook.

Its bound flight its other lit lantern its limit its flight.

Arms are raised.
Force is taken
Rain is saved. Arms are ridden the sky desecrated the sky
forsaken the loss of intelligence everywhere everywhere the
vibration in the hands that could not be raised.

A drawing and a paper and a match
A close up on the drawing.
Music in its last moments.

I saved this to write about. I gave my arms my voicebox my
lectern for spine
I gave my books for a tongue
All the walls smeared stolen charged.
Disconnected in their sheer visibility.

To walk out onto a stage like that.

The line taken extended.

The closet
The basement
The bed

The projection
The prison
The portend

The crying. In the walk extended.

Testimony talk. Tongue transplants a disease that ravaged the organs the body in just one day.

All line extended replaced by nothing.

And the nerve endings that had to be forced.

You choke on address. You limit the body you burn the sun you plant the left over seeds you wait. You linger address as it closes as the boat rocks and rocks as the fluidity is planted deep in the night. Toward what toward when.

You leave the plane the left over articles of food. You do not get married. Disconnected in your sheer visibility. You do not sleep with the sun. You lie on a bank and wait.

In the bucket of I
The absence of you
The curtailing of we

The death of them

In the turn away of that is complete.

You buy flowers and plants. You steal notebooks. You go to the
library till the very last day. The humiliation of this. The courage
of this. The evaporation. Till the very last day you find roots.

In the stolen jagged notebooks you breathe on death. Death
opens it is a flower but not for you. You are:
I stop talking
You start seizing
You lie waiting.

Death to death water to chatter. The recovered chemicals the charter.

Catheter charter

Heart
Beat.

In the stolen notebooks you write the returning of we. Nausea

becomes pronounced. The pages become globe. The fingers stop
wearing.

In the forest
The minerals
The small unannounced.

The basin the letter.

And then blank and blank and blank. Each time a name....the
empty entry extends.

Each time a door choking on breath.
The earth was soot and then cleaved
The minors wore their fingers off.
There were last letters
They said minor things.

From deep in the earth
In Praia da Luz
In Amsterdam
A heart beating a forest.
And the new words that creek in. Each word a barricade each
word a senate. Each word a seismic other held below breath
which is a phrase from before.

You followed what was foreign to you.

You held the non book to your chest.

Your wet and blue black book. But it is empty too gold as well.

And the ocean mirrors just coldness

Deep in the earth on the uncharted floor you wait.

I take that hand

I take that non hand.

What is truly a palm and cavity.

That hand in the sky about blue.

You say that you want to be more than a human being can be. Everything.

Less and more.

More

Less

The sky refuses to shut.

You untie your roots you drag them with you. Some fray. This is

to be expected. You douse your books you bury your flame.

Pristine you are prostrate against the sky as it refuses to halt.

The less that is spoken.
The more that is taken.

Book after book and article
Dedication after a dungeon so called.
And the engine this creates.
A stamp of stasis
An address

That less would be given
That more would be taken.

You wrap your book in a white sheet. You wrap your sky in
a smooth bag. You unlock the mast and the form the freeing fence.
Everything untangled. You offer your content you bury your
body you offer your break. The bark that falls now so laughable
now so desired.

It was so soft.

You sleep in this voice. You carry this secret. You contain this promise.

As the organs grow so does the body imagined
As the organ grows so does the net seizing size.

Alphabet

Eclipsed.

rebroken

A beautiful written absolute. A garden.

Some words carry more than others.

You stop binding size.

Limit eclipsed and star drawn in.

How do I get back to the other garden

There is a flood

In the flood you are kept from your body. Thus you are kept from your city. You are not with your city as it floods. The library with new pockets. The projections that would be never again. What a river would carry. I knew that it could carry this much you say proudly as you watch through gauze the books trashed translated, gone. What a line would flow what a body would border what a city can seize.

You are not with your city as it drowns.

This though is an afterthought.

You are too busy pasting too busy reading about glue.

Your house is not hit. Your gaze stays pronounced.

The files crash the fault line freezes. You dream of Alaska.
The future begs the library repays. You sell book after book.
You stop, book after book. You stop being able to read. And
especially your self.

Retention which means left back in a vocabulary long demolished.

How to say that there is no more philosophy.

To the wind I could say this but the wind is also away.

The future crashes the other sleeps. You paste stars and sleep.
Some of the glue between the pages. You are okay with this.
Everything off the table. Glued to dry. Too much glue though
and there is rejection repudiation stoppage break. Too much glue

and you might loose skin. Or you might loose article. The wind
in your sternum breaking up.

The calling IIIIIII as blocks of concrete that do not know how to fall.

You search for the other.
You send a tile.
You were not with your city as it drowned.

The books are filed a case against you. This is a language I do
not know how to speak you say when pressed.

You are too busy pummeling the glue to show up in court.

You have a visitor
On your visitor you write white into blue.
You drink stasis.
The river falls retwisted. You watch it twist your legs in the air.

You dream of a fire of a walk backward of flush.
You are brought to a city you search for an other. You retrieve
your drawing. You utter your arms. Life rafts are given out:
keepsakes. You fold yours. You have not a right to it and it is
other to you. Pronunciation is easy. A mouth no longer your own
tied to such a system. Sewage and the case against you.

You begin to waver. You access your gamble. You prayed in the
garden you removed your life vest. In the garden you were naked
in your secret as it drowned.

The shame at not being able to plant.
Or water.

You have no legs you have no legs this is a metaphor. You
redress this metaphor unleash it. It burns but you stay away from
the fire. You did not start it. The basin is not your own .

Your arms retwisted your stasis rebroken your lungs removed.

In the safety of the other body.
I drew a house
I drew a well

I was eight years and then old. Older than the mountain I stood on.

The water rushed against you. It felt good like that. The water
carried current. Current that made your mouth dry.

A speech replayed.

I wore your speech I carried your body I wove your name. You
listed my hearing. You hoarded my name. I collected your
secretion. You damaged no name. All hope dangled. You

abraded the others you wandered in court yards you followed the prison you asked for your name. You wanted in court yards. I dangled your name. You ate and ate. Sucked and spoke.

Your content inspected. A they respoken. You gathered no words. The content as expected in flame. The content as suspected eroded. The content subsumed in stasis already spoken and released.

And the holes and the journeys the corruption. Society whispered through form.

Form that was unforging, unforgiving.

You tie your neck to the boat. You tie your arc to the port. You don't look back. If you did you would never continue already swollen to twice your size. And poetry?

The journey was forgotten.

From the holes in the journey.

You are told that you must pay for your content in form.

You imagine other

You sleep in your basin

A fountain

You arrest the holes

The fountain restarts.

We were making progress this from other speech.

The porch is played with the other imagined the bowl is set.

You imagine other—what form do I have to give.

Deep in the earth the magnetic lovers.

The earth hot the earth fired. The spring water in your mouth.

All the language left unfired smooth

In the river the shapes being smooth becoming slit.

What was over, written.

And if a text is a kiss this is my last. To put you to sleep to bring you to present to charge you outside.

THE SECOND DAY

After I write I hand you this folded up paper or maybe you take
it. You take it and meet it and cram it tight.

When something is incubated it becomes precious in the absence
of tape of rhythm of notes and notation. An I that is created out
of this pocket. We smooth out the matted and leaf strewn
and sticky bits. We breathe inside. Book. Break. I.

But it could be anywhere this celebration incensed burning.

The word below that one the words inside those. Like casing.
You teach me to suck on the shell. And finally: matter.

Beside what drained. Beside what I had yet be.

For this to be a poem,

A long poem so much that I could say poem after

But the concrete comes with its own stench its own ripe and
ripped through pardon.

The difference between a waterfall and concrete this body of
mouth.

It was not reading. It was taking in. It was not dying
it was existence very deep.
Against a wall a bed a blanked out present.

I did not even fold. You did this for me.

We carried our piles of paper on the subway the areas the parks.
We practiced love. My mouth to your book. Your body to my book.
The books touch this sun.

Beyond your body what was a perfect pile. A sedimentary stature.

If I could break it to get to you.

You came to me on the plane. You came so early. Brown and
blue. So tired to get to you. The earth began to seep into text.

It was ripped though its own pardon.
Become dried

Maybe I left the paper so long in your body. So long that it became gold or it burned or became waste. What of the text that came out did you keep.

It is 2000 and. There is no reception space. The white room gone up in flames. Flames that would not carry. As you carried me as I made of you a disc.

Press and weep and space. A space so deep that nothing calls to it.

Arms dislocated from body. Waste distanced from weeping. How far would go toward that which you are not. How much would you carry to there.

Beside what drains.

Or the heavy tongue separate the parched performance the sea animal white enormous—one part of its body against the one bed wall left the other decaying in matter uncovered. There is this space and it is so deep. So deep that it can't be covered.

I crept to you. You let me in
You crept to me
I we said—I

You began to collect tongues. You placed them to dry on a piece of paper rolled out. We burnt incense. Lavender from an organic farm but really from another body. We arranged the tongues. Again and again, change and trance. I worried that they would become drained out. I bought a basin I bought another basin. We did not use them. As in my childhood I sprinkled them with water—this was so that things could be kept.

Your body language so much so that there were no words to approach it. All text started with your name. Later all text stopped with your name. You who taught me to stay to breathe to collect. At the first letter of your name an awareness that I had a hand a freeing and a freezing of a book written in distillation. A betrayal.

Your baby body
Your toddler body
Your skin unraveling.

To resist the cataloging which saves nothing which petrifies everything and who could live with these animals half consumed on the walls. These mountains of books subsumed. Even if they came out. What are they. What is this now. Out of whose body this relentlessly formed permanently formless. I traveled very far to you. To collect you.

In writing silence is first. By not writing I was saying first: you.

Because the pronouns have already been wiped out.

In the Devastation everything disappeared.
Except one.
Except once.

There were workers clearing and cleaning the throats the stacked
speech the breathing through ventilators but really it was another
body an elevator an animal in two rooms. They say clearing. We
choose nothing.

What was in I that you hoped to contain.

As covering for matter as a way to prolong its unavailable life
form we wrapped it in ambivalence neutrality. Nothing we said.
Our toppled piled pardon of nowhere.

In the present post matter—what

You had a tongue that leaked.

I did not. This was the difference.

In writing such poverty cavity calm. I watched the tenses burn, my pale orange dress up in flames. You slept through it perfectly blue perfectly brown. Your face candle ready. Sleep.

In the sea-wreck anchors were discovered boats of all kinds. It was an afterthought. It mattered to no one. Life was the rallying point. Trying to find the life in the sea creatures covered over with such depleted inscription. Existence. A force of their own dead or alive very much dead or very much alive to the point neither because there were no words for this and the mirror box holding the texts was lost in time.

Bequeathed to time. I held you out. I choked you through. You vomited and the form was freeing. I tried to vomit but I did not want to loose you. Your baby body bigger and bigger what I was hoping to contain.

What we made of cracked stone

What we made of strewn relief
The acid and the insistence
The prescription and the assumption

I lulled you to sleep. You slept.

I walked away from the cloth door. You met me half way a
spring. As I was here you put your papers together your acid in
the sun. You gave me this radiance. Moving unearthed in time
from the cloth door to the half stamped out sun. We made ties we
made rings. We walked we read. A system outside of system
outside of fusion. Our steps very important very pronounced
cracking time.

You bloomed so big.
I ate cabbages and lettuce and tomatoes green and yellow from
the garden split eigh ways, paths. What else did I take from
that garden? Of what are those nutrients now. Do they exist.
Those Saturday mornings outside of trap. A very rhythmic ocean
an endeavor. I can control the ocean you boasted. You did and
were lovely doing so. We watched our pages float out of order
flush against bloom.

You read the end. You spat in my hair in my drawer. You said I
am giving you my spit. Coquish for someone else.

Whose sun.

The fears that could become folded the evaporation that reached
the end.

Left for dead and was it something that one of us wrote or was it a necklace out of the paper a clipping that strayed to die.

So many discoveries.

There are many people who take advantage of the Devastation Boats are sold. Bartered by shape. A pea shape a pod. To lug debris. And the person who has the most debris will be the most full of language later. When the water comes back they will penetrate the sum. Life and name in one.

So many discrepancies
The water will come back.
The water is in the other bodies
The water killed itself
The water will never come back. We will die lapping after it.

A banality was split
A future was recovered

How to say how much the lovers mourned and the sympathy I feel for them pushed flush against language with nothing in their mouths.

The water books so meaningful they cannot be. In refrain. On a
standing frame.

The economy larger and larger
The events smaller and smaller
A narrative mouth perdition exploitation cover and close.

I wanted an end to this circuit and so I decided to take it inside.
This sea life
This matter
A place where all things fronted form

As the bodies shot into space.
As the elements tried
As the curtains returned
The absence curtailed
You crumpled that poison letter having finally learned how to
read
You slashed the bed instead of the throat
The wave lines split
To have content instead of form
The trap of the prison the public the seismic the met
Cataloged as prior previous before.

You trumped that frozen letter
And as form the poison

Stuck in the bank as area
A blanket over your chest drawing you to nothing

The search instead of your mouth
Those hands instead of your pocket

Searching.

To have form instead of constancy matter
This is what has been drowned out
This is what I have to give you
These empty cisterns.
In the sky radiant
In the content tried

After the Devastation we tried to eat form
But it was unclear what it was to swallow.
Shallow is that a word
Remembrance as gesture
As dye overdeveloped
A tie in somebody else's water
A salve over somebody else's burn.

To whom does my skin belong
For whom was the desert saved
For whom was it starved.

Shallow is that word that later that body unprepared for such
evacuation of matter
For the cries of
Water in vomit
Water in content
Water in an agreement to narrative.

Before they drained us or cleaned us or made us a fish they said testify.

Shallow is a water that seems to have survived being.

I wanted your body of water your blue and brown endeavor.

There was nothing that was unprepared in you wrung out in you.

Narrative casing Russian dolls a water pit a fire a hell. Sobs stolen.

We thought the hell would be shared
We though the rubble would be met
A barricade for whom for what.

Shallow is a water

Very sparse very strained
The herb garden
The demolition sites
The library.

And the people who still say overseas.
Who still pocket entire
A commitment to nothing
To netting terribly untainted untried.

One day when you could not sleep you read some of my text. It
was on the computer in the white room where we slept. This
voice dragged to me today. With what words of praise. They
were full they were effusive they were as singular as you and
they are empty today. Still your voice in this net an unbearable
fact of being.

This voice drags me to today. The shyness of it the pronounce of
it. And I imagined dragged behind it name and after shell.
Scream and after softness. Sacrosanct—You left your staff you
left your rake.

The imaginings how strained this life sifted so thin.

Shallow is this water which finds itself here.
Nets made out of names doors forgotten skin

By the same people who steal and shelter blood
Blood echoers book sustainers.
It was named after you they say your lost name as they try to
convince you to part with your skin.

What did I think that writing was?

It was not now.
It was not shared
It was pure as that room was pure
A purity that escaped being

The way you would make the room all lit
The many cathedrals
The icons
The entrees the entireties
Such a soft glow swallowed water

You wanted me to die with you. Before the crisis, when it was
just us alone. You wanted me to drown with you. Our hearts
water met. Weather tried. Was this written. You said I exposed
the room. I sent you curtains in the mail incense in the mail I
would have sent myself should have sent myself.

My love and my bereavement you wanted me to die with you

So cold the water in your heart and then my stone as I tried to
seize against it.

A purity that escapes.
A faucet you said
And so this my announcement my gift my belonging
A silence that would not demean entry.
Writing became what was to be stolen. Silence became what was to be kept.
A bag of silence out of which dust shook

You did not accept my words. Or you did not accept them
drowned in voice you kept your own counsel and my own words.

But because you were in me you accepted my silence. Our code
word our language the ravaged city put to sleep. Decimated and
desired. In your bag of stars what is it that means: accept?

The way you lit each word each book each regret.
My tangled throat like everybody else's—growing things
A choked and strangled water.
Stagnant a word we could accept.

Silence a word we could betray.

What was beyond the barrier resilience. No one knew and all
were quiet, silent.
We were so proud of our throats.

The way you lit each match a frozen city.

The most beautiful word throat. A decaying ocean a microcosm of calm
and fluidity. The reason we could still say: I

In the absence of address

Everyone IIIIII.

My throat. My avenue

My mountain of memory

And who could cry the most. If this could ever be addressed.

There are the lovers still and what shades them.
They are unlooked at
They are unwatched.
My throat is so tangled!

A people torn out of language
A tension torn out of time
Permission.
And its base
Its dawn its upheaval
Its lights.
For all those carriers of water blinking their eyes trying to speak.

I gave you that year.
I emptied my books.
Look at it the water in thin passage following itself
I tipped the books into your river your prison pond
Yes, you said. Yes.

A wave so small draining itself
The banded seahorse
And then
Sea
And then horse

And then sea

Hooves

And lack

The Namers like meteors.
The heavy and starched attempts at new language.
The dialects remembered by The Namers
Crammed open
Splayed with stolen throats.
It is for the good of all don't be so selfish open your mouth

You might be Jesus. He too a fish.

Capable of water

Waling on water. I want to swim.

Don't wail. You will not be joined.

Instead you should wander the earth.

Your throat to share.

Your beautiful letters

My book

I need this notebook inscription for my book.
It was shallow where it was found
Plundered
Etched in blood.
Not everyone has your water.
Brevity a silence a bereavement.

The namers thinking that they are Jesus.

The hair split open like everyone else.

There were many different kinds of assonances water.
It was impossible to speak them all at the same time
And yet they were lit
He
She
I and you. It was said. All these things crammed into speech.

You lit this for me.

Bare and braced. The plumage undone.

Beside what held
Beside what drew
Beside what had yet to be

In all the water suctioned and met—the world

Why would this matter

A poverty of thought

In line.

Part Four: THE BASIN

A long time ago I was drawn, along with you, on a cave wall, and with you I have swam from its dark depths down to today

—*Clarice Lispector*

As light as a tree this, the trunk so powerfully rooted.

I limp to you I come toward you.

You are wet.

I limp to you you are tired
You say you are tired
I make vials of our colors our lining
Wet silk craved
It falls the silk falls I will never reach the ladder

All the people dying in their place the fumes the revolutions the carnivals
the containers. The return. Bark as sick as day.

Vials for our enclosures our pockets of air.
Flames for our filters. Our stops. These jugs of air.

And there is no commitment in entire in the seaming of silk in the envelope that floors in the small lining that breaks following. This billowing tree trunk. Where does it attach to what does it attach. Of what reason is air and to whom do I write.

The lost consensus. The plain air. The torn air the air that is split storm by sky. Mesh spirit wing censor flight. All these things forgiven. As I fly to you. As I ask you to pick out all the glass lining my entire wrapped in lost flight, its wings.

There is the seaweed that comes out of you. This I do not pick off. This just comes. You leave this and I carry it. Soon I will eat it to make a space for you.

At the bottom of the sea unannounced there is no tide

There is no structure

The sea that I carried for you, the sea that I made for you.

The entire bigger than words which are separate discrete and overfull of boundaried matter clinging to a substance without layer. The buried limits the hard sentences the non cave.

From the outside there is the image.

From the inside nothing. My hand could be my throat and nothing belongs to me. Not you and not this structure that has ruined us.

I lit a match
I found a tree
You were not there.

I come toward you. I stop I wait. I come toward you. The ocean leaks.
The brevity slackens. The ocean waits. The cold that is reflected
becomes mineral.

Everyday the limp passage toward nowhere. A language that does not
combine. A regret that is written as stop a telegram in a war. The birds
decayed and used. The oceanic decamped. The surfeit ingested. Too close.
And everything coming at once and which way to go. To trust that there is
nothing to stop that there is something. The night falls. The blade is shut.
The arm're appears.

No one wants to choke on a body. The slight variations that mean time
that mean resistance. Resistance reliance resilience of the smallest kind.
The tearing down the argument and the known noun, the building back of
the entire.

To make a pile. A blade a leaf a very hard place. And then all one thing. To
be decamped there. The multiple metastasis freeing. The earlier in your ear
your air. The telegrams abated. The stasis resunken. The blades resown.

Writing to add to pile writing to accentuate wall. To decorate to decamp to
be on the inside where the shooter is. The small window in the door. The
bird bodies flinging themselves. The steps halfway, the multiple pardons.
A long list not a garden

Not a dragged to here. This clean break.

To testify to sorrow, to build a cell again and again. One cell block by block. And for the building to press hard against matter. So hard that it is impossible to see.

The meaning doesn't change the value doesn't change. What changes is that it is another day like this and I is recorded and it is bound and the brevity the engorgement is complete.

That there is nothing left there.

That the telegrams will have no meaning later. That the bird bodies will not be buried will not be flame. They will be washed up in the water that is left. The dirty water now tied to here.

To make a list of sorrow. Or not sorrow an erasure that is planted stark clean. Nothing was dragged to here

As you swim out of the broken net this is what you find.

I come to you without scales without language to the immeasurable part of you that I put beside water.

.

At the bottom of the sea there is nothing.

A book that could be but isn't.

For the dead matter

For the matter that lives

And for the water

The gorges the centenaries the ashes the muffins the amber. That hair, those infusions protections, oversights. Those injunctions. Walking that very far fine line toward nowhere.

The life that was enclosed. The lines that were returned retied—refused. A referendum.

Everywhere debris. No clear space. No singular species. No water alone.

How easy it was to draw a wave.

In the throats of the lovers was something that was always there. It just grew larger.

An infusion an infection all that refused to break. A terrarium but terrible tangled—and beautiful. But only when seen in very wide shot. A photograph I saw long ago. A photograph torn of a book. But more tired than that too. And the water threatening even this.

To choke on your own species to draw your own line. Maybe it was I wanted to die. But not through the cracks. In the earth yes there was a basin and they never lay down. Three years later it is this same gesture. This image torn of a book.

This was still skin.

An arm reaches

A pavement judges

The sky rehearses

And we are speaking for whom.

The first day of speaking after an area uncovered. You got old so quickly. There was a sky. I practiced. All the front lines removed. The boredom, the resuscitations the narrative. We do not practice together. We who are waiting—for whom.

I wanted further it is true. The water got so big. It practiced speaking. I wanted further even after the frost. The earth abated. The lining was dug out. My park was packaged.

It used to be that writing held.

I sat in the basin and it covered me.

One dead lump to another. One dead time freeing the other for whom for when. You climbed over the rubble on the porch of the house where you lived. You have waited nine years and now it is just the demolition. I could lick the walls and they would turn to ice. To stand there.

How is it that the lovers survived.

Those who did not are unspeakable

I reach through this partition to touch them but the touch is unpardonable and the recoiling now has weight.

It was like this: memory. For so long.

It was a different thing to write all over thinking things would be kept. Now to brush against this:

Or this:

And everything else that got so lost.

I don't even know if it was cold there.

Sometimes it seemed as though you could write the book for me.

You would give me things. You would answer me through the frost. It would come from elsewhere that which you said.

These things against my skin would answer a question.

Open a question.

I had an idea of making the book like that all this misreading from start to finish and the empty question inside. A book just for me. And for you who have no name.

We don't gather things. Even—we. It is left. I choked a long time. Too long to gather.

It was cold in the inside and on the pavement. Nothing came together.

It is a different bed a different time.

Before poetry made the separation.

The poetry bound to here and to the water gathered up in time.

There are not arms big enough.

Over me, the sweeping gestures you make.

The nausea that becomes pronounced. The biting into syllables, the inhaling into speech. The decaying into matter. The matter not alone. Thrice tried.

The disorder that molted and the time it took to die.

What did I take off you
What did I give you
What is it that I left you

Your body made of rocks
Your body made of chemicals

Be feathers

A salvage, marked

—How can one write a one book?

—One picks up a heavy sheet of ice. One slips and falls.
One evades the presence in oneself these heavy winds
which become book. One dies and that is the fire.

—Of what of the grief of the lost things?

—Grief is also an object, resplendent and full of holes. I
wanted to water that which was not there. The partitions
fell. There was no matter.

—How can I write this book without you?

—Writing is alone. It is the skin separate, the fruit. What
the skin bore in order to survive.
> The earth that is shed of me.
> The earth that is separate from me.

> You, who are unimaginable.

—What season is it now?

—Now it is winter.

In the depth of the image I look for light.

It was so bloody.

If in the basin there is chalk instead of water.

Sometimes I feel in hunger that my body is in all separate languages. It is up to you to translate them into the same language and then bring them to feeling. Pull them together. I know that only you could so this for me and there is pleasure to think of the tension in your mouth the curves and the sown dialects. There is also your own language. Which parts this. All or none, I don't know. Maybe something so small a blocked mirror. Pleasure also at these small blocks in your mouth addressing.

Only then would I be able to feel.

Then you could kiss me and I would feel it. Then you could pour me or make me a safe and I would be able to feel the fire beneath me, that which lies still.

It is so heavy the steps, broken by crumpled paper, newspaper even.

Your watch stops. Your climate hazards. Your seismic becomes undone

I watch you, all of you throat. That which I reached to place here.

The theater empty the sun undone.

The gutter empty, the urns undone. Such powder.

Alone in the street reaching for this.

I lay next to the space in you that is empty that is cold.

This film in the air.

These bones in the stream.

So rapt. So stopped.

We follow the route until we are caught
How long the journey to here.

On the clean lawn, the billowing sheets.

In the clipped bed aspects of sea

In your hair a wave to be tied.

A front to be forced: tide.

There could have been another book. The book that was already written. I would just salvage it. Meaning and its separation. On the floor and on the ceiling of the sea.

You wrote this book with me. But I can't take your words.

Still I touch these aspects and there is sorrow for the meaning that would be in the combination in the recombination. The debris stacked. The debris spread out. The debris reconstituted—through.

There is not any wavering.

There is meaning and its pronunciations.

The rules of debris very pronounced

I touch your fur. I touch your translation. Your book.

The time after rubble if something so decayed can be called that. A wall. A block. An ink mouthing graffiti. But nothing the mound could hold.

It was summer then it was lake. We were scorched and fighting with the others.

The composite rotted.

Bound

How to say that I tore the globe I watched it unravel the star chart in flames.

And that I would never drown in a river only the ocean.

What did we see of skin.

Seawreck impossible to press against.

How to trace this angel.

How to get close enough. The river tips the stones dissolve the angel loses its head. This is a metaphor that does not trace

There is the dust. Deep in the ground. such stars on your tongue. The certainty. Smooth half moons a strain. Dirty water caught in a jar a jet bowl. Where once leaves

The future stained

The cloth does not balance the sky the nothing stays to dry, the articles are hung—smooth star. And in the sky there is ancient.

Walking the stone steps down and down and down into a plate that is broken.

Already where does it fit in the whole what can be lost for the whole. As though the gesture does not matter. The tip back of the head. The elegant fall. The search back of the surety. The dust that spoke the ocean that rang. Your skin so close.

In the hour before dust. In the time before rain. In the ocean outside of met.

A swamp of strain. Slowly draining itself or giving. It is hard to tell as it mixes with the rain the heat this memory of ocean entire.

Still you are awake at this time.

I hung you. You dazzled me. You ate this star. There were star parts in your lungs, shards of share and light. I hugged you. You are fire you said. I measured you there were small parts bits. A notebook from before. Bark, something green. Star parts ash hung. We swept into the fire. The bottle was wept. All light dazzled. It was snow. Maybe this will be the water. The trees great ash and the vision complete. Image where you lay across blank page. The park deserted. The park restrung. A trust in bottle and finishing blindly. I did kiss that tree. I did drown, that vapor. It was cold. You poured me. The ash shook. The fire spoke the ceiling cleared. All lungs deserted. Such light, this.

I crouched to where you where.

I put my lips to that tongue that shell.

There comes a day when you touch it. This separate this dissolve. You touch it. As something rises. Hollow hard stone. Which to pick which to choose. All meaningful or meaningless hard litter. It could be anywhere it could be nothing. With one finger. Gingerly, but no hesitation. Is/it.

We remember tears. Which come fresh but are not for sale. Which come flush but stop. Memory, just before extinction.

The innocence in the abundance the certitude in the sale the miracle in all the measure the starting to clear. It is green it has the look of algae if it were not so late. I remember when you used to say—and here.

Impoverishment. Is there abundance there. My hand is for you but also has no meaning. I come to you without scales without language. We do not embrace. A stone is a thing that cannot be filled. Nor the bottle nor that storm that rose. The innocence in the inscription the many kinds of assonances water. All hollow jug. It filled.

You crack. You roll in the vapor the shade. Such wave: shade. It is a shock. The seaweed builds and builds. So many cloth doors. You track. And writing takes you....Behind this big stone. At the edge of the rolled map the newly pronounced grass. The regraspable straw the ocean and the lemon. The ceiling and the fire. This furnace protruding. Because I just want to be here and that is the only reason why.

To write to the sky (open, deneutered) is different from writing to you. The notebook closed and become blue.

I will never be able to get close enough to what is real.

The star cracks
The ocean floor

If you stayed beyond a season.

We put our books in a cloth bag. This is a door. Our tide goes where. The floor flushes the arms accept this earth. The terms that have been smuggled in the hearing listed the stems re-appropriated the ocean slept. I wanted to sleep this way but it kept moving. The cloth door the German books the stamped out sun.

For it to be okay that there is not a never. The stems so tied. The stars so slit. The ocean unbounded. The waves unlit. The season so squeezed. Nothing ran. For this to be okay.
Strain.
How to show this.

Through the cheesecloth through the article the fire. The words hard against the rubbing board. The stones low in the river so late. The basin I left there the forever tried there the ocean accept and the tie that was such tongue.

I am afraid to go backward like this. These rooms now dark and empty.

And the only real water: that this cannot be enough that you are not where I left you. That the snow will not melt and the season will not try. That your pockets are not deep enough nor your words bare enough. I dream of walls and not a basin. You go on carrying this debris because it is not allowed that our cataloging would make a pattern. Otherwise there would never be a name. I put my lips to yours:

And yes that this is outside of world.

For a long time it was just in the front as figural. Then at the same moment as an awareness of time the face your hair. To take without ripping. To distinguish the matted from the shade. To get closer to the essence that had fallen behind it self. All this faded. As the sun eclipsed itself and all that we were burning to see.

Sometimes you take from me slower. Hold something. (Hold long sigh memory breath) distinguish it from the rest. I let it fall. Once on the floor it will enter back into the concrete. I do not have this discernment. The brevity too split. The sun too piled. The scent too pallid. For now.

Because you do not speak it becomes fall but I know from your gesture that it could become globe.

I took from the dream what could not be caught. I folded I planned I released. The frames swam, the curvature buckled the century seized. This is late century someone says. But really it is early. Untainted and until stained. The cloth could not hold. It was not meant to. I lay my head against your cloth heart. Which moved. I fingered entire. I forgot the sentence My head a bag of stones. The sentence was magic. It opened the door.

And for whom is there also water.

There is the sun in front of them. The sun that won't burn. How round. Such smooth—word.

There is the ache in this part the obscuring century the bullfrogs jumping out of the lake.

As though someone tore them but from what from where when they are just so close.

No one will know what happens to them on the other side the gestures that stayed to die. Or to live. Does this continue does this un-continue the essential failure of language the book that I cannot give them.

In passage through the sun

If I were another person I would be able to write a beautiful book. For them. And translate its water through the sun.

But there is this I and it is unmet.

You do not know:

That my skin is repairing itself. That the work is slow.

That I stopped dreaming of glue that I separated the outside that no pot will ever be met that there are paints in the earth that the skin is fired that the bowl is so hot.

That it is uncomfortable to lie down in the basin alone.

Such grief to get to the beginning. There it was. The last fall the last winter. Such stark whiteness. The lace unfurled uncaught. I enter that door that glass. I press that key. The water from my face. The dryness from my stomach. The upheaval. Every door signaled the end. And the earth that had betrayed me something so fall, nature and language in the park the entry, stream. Still I went each day. Still I collected being. I cost love in all the many stomachs. It was the beginning of all the prying open. But for now you are skinned lying on the white couch a blanket. It is night. There are many candles they drift.

The blue which was white had given over to brown. Everyday I wore the duster that became later the gift part of your story. There it hangs in a house painted over high up. A last attempt: lavender. There they sat. There they loved. There I walked you to work. There they dream. As though a skin repairing itself. These tendrils released. Something so dry that has no cost. There you emptied. There you called: the sky. This boundlessness. The joy that you gave me that grief that you saved me from. And if our constellations touched it was silent.

In the beginning it was plain your blue cups on an oven floor. Later it was embellished. But not the walk. The one name that is real to me.

Pure sound.

I climbed out of the bed, the matter.

Courage falls to the ground.

I give you this charred earth this damaged root. To do with it what you will.

How to restore gift. Beside what dangled and the contagion that falls.

One person moves toward another person. Many years after person had been introduced. It is heat. A person wears black and white is weary. A person wears green and brown is nervous and like a light. A person is like a sieve. There is an opening that moves. There is a fire that takes. A train that removes all night. There was that solitary tree that solitary self. What did they speak of. There is something unformed in a person. This represents great passion. There is something dimly lit. There is the growing garden of weeds. A backward glance you say.

As they meet one on the ground, caught one in the sky, borrowed. If they could speak they would say we make a star. But luckily they cannot speak (don't speak!) and I still have to go to that burial in the air and there is still the rock to be carried the soft bundle so brief. What radiated was so small. Debris I would say if I had touched I then but life was a slot and so small. One person passes: another. This becomes language. This gesture.

How to restore gift.

I listened most closely to that which I did not understand.

Existence. Is it singular does it move. What happened to it in the bucket.

There was such freedom if you listened too deep.

I resolved to carry that which was not there.

Slowly they move up the tree.

It was important for you to choose death. In death I choose you any you. And the body. Subsuming the narrative that continued it was so trampling so blunting. In I there are molecules of we. A we that is difficult to pronounce.

That there would be space for each person. That no one is replaceable. That no one contains a light that could be shared stamped or silenced off.

In choosing death which became metaphorical in a room that disdained metaphor I was saying shadow and the proof that the shadowing extras gave.

The world lost forward. I lost all those years.

.

There were too many things done with books. The Namers became bloated huge, huge rays of chemicals, fortified with the privileged water caught.
Life they said.

It was not pure
It was not abstract
There was no material to speak of.

That I no longer know how to write a book. That a book is a world. That much of the world is lost desired deserted drained. Turned over. That there is a void in the world a void in the word. That it cannot be seen.

They did look like life.

Do I catalog all the debris which would take many years and the daily risk of confronting non meaning or do I just finger one small pile. It was all indistinguishable. Even to make a path a perch a private setting so much had to be discarded, there were bits of meaning in the non meaning I know. Essential a word from before.

There was so much that was mangled so much infected with fleas. I could not kill the mice that crawled over time. The passage narrow dark and cramped. So many toxins already. I knew that there was not room to add more. Another sunburst. Another death. The performance that was preventative.

That I no longer have a feeling for language. That it could be this or it could be that and is there abundance in all impoverishment. Without the other I mean the one to call it forth. And if so how to discard how to face this flight this wreckage this sun so behaved and frightened, slipped. I slipped that disc into your hand. You crawled to me. The space is larger.

The specificity is what made the lovers survive. Even outside of language they were specific they were themselves they held the void between them they coveted their tears. In another life I gave you a table. It is okay that this comes in.

Parched throats. Dangled hopes. Redressed entries.

To search through all that non meaning for meaning. And how each clings one to the other. Separation without the mirror box. Surgery knowing that it is damned.

There are many images of them. They float to the imaginary surface dreaming of them. They sit before a blue glass wall. They sit beside a green stone fence. The horses trample them. The turnstile turns them the ocean clots their breezes. If it were more safe if something had been saved I could pull a letter from my palm.

For/you.

The wager that had been torn.
The turn away from water.
The blown away gestures. Acquiesced

Under the bed that you made.

Under a book no longer a bed.

The draught veins the dusty chemicals the poison in your mouth.

The distance shallow—swallow.

The couriers again and again

The breach of life

The salt of death

What this very strong light means.

When you are so hungry. When the world closes in. Remembrance of perfection. I said that I looked back it fell. Remembrance of repository that fall. I ached for what was not there.

That I have not the range I had or the force even of last week.

That time cannot be divided.

That nothing stands to close

That here we are,

Objectless, hurled a force taken.

In the basin was

The lovers do not choose. They are.

The lovers do not bathe; they bring.

The air sweeps them, the fire seals them the rivers burn their covers.

A confidence in all that lost speech now dismembered remembered un-torn un-teamed.

There is no I that chooses.

There is no I that I choose

That there is now just this one book. Just this one disembodied stone.

What is a noun on its own a voice on its own.

I could search forever and not find it.

The ache that was lost in time the refuge from the water itself.

The salt making roots

The roots sprawling

A world taking place too fast

Then it was that I could not leave this place.

Roots distangled of other roots

The salt at first substance, matter

Then a rigid pelvis, legs

 Later

That which was in no book.

The clarity an irregularly shaped time. Or time unwept.

I stopped collecting things.

I stopped being able to remember where I left things found things.

Ragged roots decay rapt around themselves

There was no main space

There was no solid entry

I turned my back and the water illusion dissolved

I put my hands in the basin.

There was nothing there.

Should we catalog the salt.

The low sound so common.

The image lasted this long. The image never left me. Now in the dark, the halved particles.

Instead of hollow space reaching for a basin reaching for a drawer.

There is the sun but no light shining.

I emptied out. There was the sea.

For they shall not forever, for mankind shall not forever, for they shall not have to wait forever.

—Ingeborg Bachmann

LAST THINGS

I wanted to speak to the book

I wanted the book to speak for me

None of these things can ever happen.

Similarly the water in the bodies of the lovers.

There it stays:

For them.

ACKNOWLEDGEMENTS

Thank you to Mei-Mei Berssenbrugge to David Buuck to Jamila Cornick to Lisa Bufano to Ofer Eliaz to Brian Evenson to Joanna Howard to Bhanu Kapil to Stephen Motika to Thelonious Rider to Juliana Spahr to Sasha Spahr to Andrea Spain to Rachel Zolf. For help with the different times of this book.

Thank you also to my students at St. John's University in Jamacia, Queens for working on meaning with me.

And to those at Naropa who did the seemingly impossible task of charging the space of debris.

Thank you also to my students at Pratt Institute who participated in the theater that was "relation class" that I co-taught with performance artist Alex Schweder.

Thank you as well to Forrest Gander and Susan Bernstein for inviting me to Brown to speak on healing and philosophy, to the editors of *Trickhouse* for featuring this book as part of a curation on proximity, to the Millay Colony who granted this book a summer stay, to CA Conrad for featuring me in his paranormal poetics series and for his enormous crystal light, to Bhanu Kapil for inviting me to be in her Naropa Symposium "Violence and Community" to Tisa Bryant who invited me to talk about these subjects at Cal Arts to Dawn Kasper who invited me to read this work as part of her durational art in the Whitney Biennial to Eleni Stecopoulos who invited me to preform in her Poetics of Healing symposiums in both Berkeley and NY and to Vanessa Place and Teresa Carmody who invited me to the Shindler House in LA to talk about negation in a place where inside and outside literally met.

The extreme interest in pronouns which runs through the entire book is indebted to Juliana Spahr's work of the last ten years. The cover image is a collaboration between Juliana, David Buuck, Andrew Kenower, and me.

Thank you to Emji Spero of Timeless, Infinite Light for designing the cover of this book. Thank you to Margaret Tedesco for designing the interior. Thank you to Stephen Motika and to Nightboat for a lot of understanding, for this great experience and for the holding down of such lovely space. I am honored to be a part of it.

The phrase "cloth heart" on page 117 is taken from Bhanu Kapil's *Humanimal* (Kelsey Street, 2009).

The italicized lines on page 33 are Alejandra Pizarnik's (first line) and Edmond Jabes' (second line).

I wish to thank Bhanu Kapil in particular—and her own books *Ban* and *Schizophrene* without which/whom my work would never have been. A friend with whom I was able to put the dead and the life so close together in a daily way that they could almost breathe—or die—again. Thank you for all the mirrors the clay shapes washing the river, the giving of existence to so many things. The negative shapes decomposing finally into something new. Fidelity as the word sun. What writing can be past waste, past exhaustion. Pre shape: a whole bound life.

This book was written in isolation although now I think that the whole work was effort to get to this beautiful line of Glissant from his *Poetics of Relation*: "We know ourselves as part and as crowd, in an unknown that does not terrify. We cry our cry of poetry. Our boats are open, and we sail them for everyone."

Thank you to everyone.

Nightboat Books, a nonprofit organization, seeks to develop audiences for writers whose work resists convention and transcends boundaries. We publish books rich with poignancy, intelligence, and risk. Please visit our website, www.nightboat.org, to learn about our titles and how you can support our future publications.

The following individuals have supported the publication of this book. We thank them for their generosity and commitment to the mission of Nightboat Books:

Kazim Ali
Elizabeth Motika
Benjamin Taylor

In addition, this book has been made possible, in part, by a grant from the New York State Council on the Arts Literature Program.